# Contents

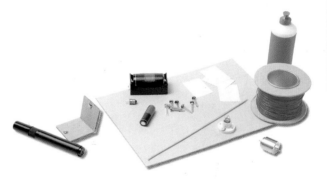

# Our electric world

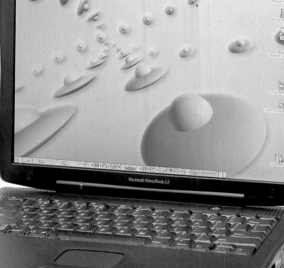

HOW MANY TIMES TODAY have you used something electric? Maybe you have watched television, listened to a radio, turned on a light, used a computer, electric toothbrush, hair dryer or even a lift. Electricity does so much in our daily lives. It is hard to believe that one hundred years ago very few homes had electricity!

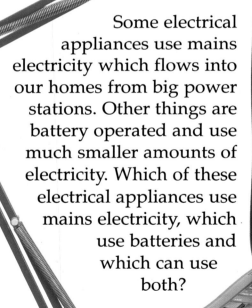

Some electrical appliances use mains electricity which flows into our homes from big power stations. Other things are battery operated and use much smaller amounts of electricity. Which of these electrical appliances use mains electricity, which use batteries and which can use both?

# Science Experiments

## WITH

# TRICITY

ivell-Aston
ny Jackson

# W
# FRANKLIN WATTS
## LONDON • SYDNEY

This edition 2003

Franklin Watts
96 Leonard Street, London EC2A 4XD

Franklin Watts Australia
45-51 Huntley Street
Alexandria
NSW 2015

Series editor: Rachel Cooke
Designer: Mo Choy
Picture research: Susan Mennell
Photography: Ray Moller, unless otherwise
acknowledged

A CIP catalogue record for this book
is available from the British Library.

ISBN 0 7496 5340 X

Dewey Classification 537

Printed in Malaysia

Acknowledgements:
Cover: Steve Shott;
Bruce Coleman p.7bl;
Image Bank p.10b;
Science Photo Library p.28b (Martin Bond);
Science Museum/Science and Society Picture Library
pp.9t, 15bl, 23b;
Sony Consumer Products Group p.25t.

Thanks, too, to our models: Erin Bhogal, Perry
Christian, Bonita Crawley, Jaimé Leigh Pyle, Jordan
Oldfield, Nicholas Payne, Jennifer Quaife and
Alexander Smale.

# Science Experiments

## WITH

...TRICITY

...ivell-Aston

...ny Jackson

## W
# FRANKLIN WATTS
### LONDON • SYDNEY

This edition 2003

Franklin Watts
96 Leonard Street, London EC2A 4XD

Franklin Watts Australia
45-51 Huntley Street
Alexandria
NSW 2015

Copyright © Franklin Watts 2000

Series editor: Rachel Cooke
Designer: Mo Choy
Picture research: Susan Mennell
Photography: Ray Moller, unless otherwise
acknowledged

A CIP catalogue record for this book
is available from the British Library.

ISBN 0 7496 5340 X

Dewey Classification 537

Printed in Malaysia

Acknowledgements:
Cover: Steve Shott;
Bruce Coleman p.7bl;
Image Bank p.10b;
Science Photo Library p.28b (Martin Bond);
Science Museum/Science and Society Picture Library
pp.9t, 15bl, 23b;
Sony Consumer Products Group p.25t.

Thanks, too, to our models: Erin Bhogal, Perry
Christian, Bonita Crawley, Jaimé Leigh Pyle, Jordan
Oldfield, Nicholas Payne, Jennifer Quaife and
Alexander Smale.

## Be amazed!

By doing the experiments in this book you will find out some amazing things about electricity. You will find out about how it lights things, moves things and makes things buzz! Some experiments may answer questions you already have about electricity, some may make you think of more!

## Look closely!

Scientists ask lots of questions and observe carefully. When you do the experiments, look closely to see what is happening and keep a record of your results. Don't be upset if your predictions are not always correct as scientists (and that includes you) learn a lot from unexpected results.

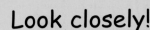

## Be careful!

Always make sure an adult knows you are doing an experiment. Remember: only do the experiments with the batteries listed (not rechargeable, which can overheat). NEVER play with appliances that use mains electricity or the wall sockets they connect to. DO NOT cut open batteries or touch car batteries. It is VERY dangerous to do any of these things and could even kill you. Follow the step-by-step instructions carefully and remember – be a safe scientist!

# See the static!

HAVE YOU EVER HEARD a crackling noise when you take off a jumper? This crackle is caused by 'static electricity'. Static electricity builds up when some things rub against each other, and it does not move through a wire. Find out more in this first experiment.

**Wear a wool jumper for good results in this experiment!**

✔ **you will need**
- ✔ a balloon
- ✔ tissue paper
- ✔ other types of paper
- ✔ scissors

**1** Cut some simple bird shapes out of the tissue paper about 5 cm wide at the wings.

**2** Blow up a balloon then rub it against your jumper to build up static electricity. You have now 'charged' the balloon.

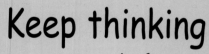

## Keep thinking

Have you ever noticed a crackling sound when you put your finger near a TV screen or when you turn it off? What do you think is causing the crackle?

**3** Now hold the balloon high above the tissue paper birds.

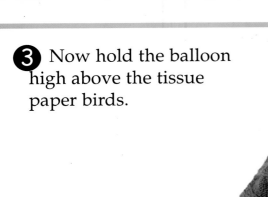

Gently lower the balloon towards them. What happens?

# In action

Lightning in thunderstorms occurs when clouds become charged with static electricity, which then sparks between the clouds or between the clouds and the ground.

**4** Now repeat the experiment using birds made of different types of paper. Make sure they are the same size as the tissue paper birds to make the test fair. What happens each time? Which type of paper do you think gives the most interesting results?

# Don't stop there

Rub the balloon against your jumper again. Can you make the balloon 'stick' to the wall? How long will it stay 'stuck' before it falls down?

# Electricity flows

ALL THE ELECTRICAL OBJECTS we use work with current electricity, not static. An electric current is made up of very small particles called electrons, which flow around in a path called a circuit. The battery in a torch pumps electrons around the circuit. Find out more in this experiment.

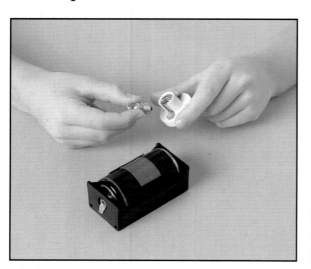

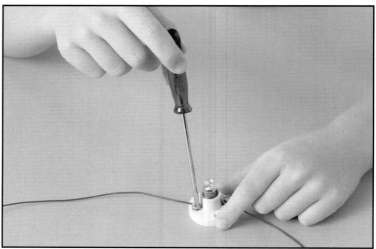

**1** Put the battery in the battery holder and screw the bulb into the bulb holder.

**2** Use the screwdriver to attach one of the stripped ends of each wire to the bulb holder, as shown.

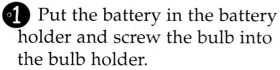

## Keep thinking

What do you think would happen if you left the circuit connected for a long time? Would the bulb stay bright forever? What are the reasons for your answer?

# In action

This is a model of the very first battery. It was made in 1800 by a scientist called Alessandro Volta. The layers you can see are zinc, copper and pieces of paper. Volta had soaked the paper in salty water. The small current that flowed was called 1 volt.

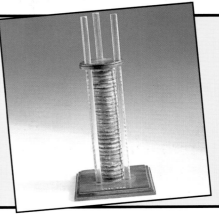

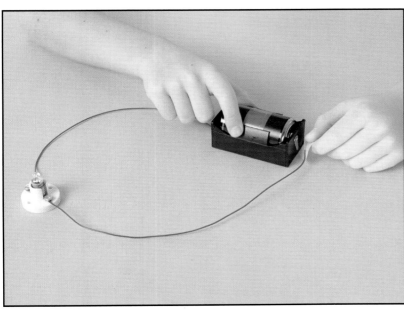

**3** Tape the other end of each piece of wire to either end of the battery holder. You have now made a simple circuit.

**4** What happens? Does the bulb light up?

**5** Predict what will happen if you turn the battery round. Will the bulb light? Test to see if your prediction was correct.

**Safety: the torch bulb gets warm when it lights up. Although a torch bulb is safe to touch, never touch bulbs on lights at home as these can get very hot.**

# Don't stop there

● Draw a picture of your circuit to show the positions of the bulb, battery and wires. What path do you think the electric current takes around the circuit?
● Find out more about batteries – for example, with a clock kit like this one. It can be powered by fruit and vegetables. It uses two metals, zinc and copper, and the juices in the fruit to make a battery.

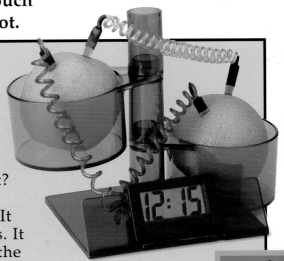

# Breaking the circuit

W̲ʜᴇɴ ʏᴏᴜ ᴡᴀɴᴛ ᴛᴏ turn a light on or off, you use a switch. Find out in this experiment how switches let an electrical current flow around a circuit or stop it.

**✓ you will need**
- ✓ simple circuit (as used in experiment on pages 8/9)
- ✓ 2 paper fasteners
- ✓ corrugated card
- ✓ piece of wire with ends stripped

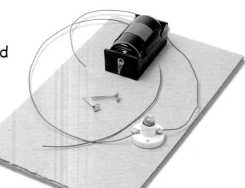

**❶** First make a switch. Cut a rectangle of card approximately 10 cm x 5 cm. Fix the two paper fasteners as shown in the picture. Fold the card in half.

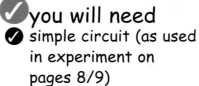

**❷** Wrap one end of the piece of wire around one paper fastener as shown.

## In action

In the past, large switches were used to cause explosions! Pressing down the switch let the electricity flow through a circuit, which lit the explosives. Switches are still used to cause explosions, but they are much smaller.

**3** Connect the switch into your simple circuit by disconnecting one wire from the battery holder and wrapping it around the other paper fastener. Then connect the loose end of the wire attached to the first paper fastener to the battery holder instead.

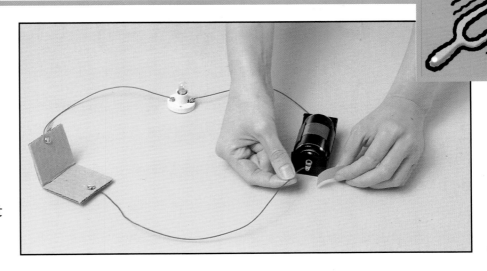

## Keep thinking

If you had a simple circuit with two switches, one open and one closed, would the bulb light up? Try making one to find out.

**4** Push the two halves of the card together so the paper fasteners touch each other. The switch is now closed. What happens to the bulb?

**5** Now release the card so the paper fasteners no longer touch. The switch is now open. What happens to the bulb? What happens to the flow of electric current each time? Is an open switch on or off?

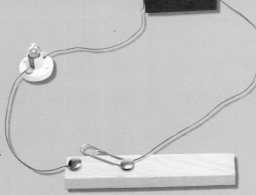

## Don't stop there

● Make another type of switch using a small piece of softwood, two drawing pins and a paper clip. Connect it into a simple circuit. How do you switch the bulb on and off?

● Look around your home or school. Make a list of all the different kinds of switch you can find.

# Bright lights?

IN A TORCH THE ELECTRIC current pumped around by the battery only has to light up one bulb. But sometimes the electric current needs to light up more than one bulb. Find out more in this experiment.

## ✅ you will need
- ✔ 2 batteries (1.5V) with holders
- ✔ 5 lengths (about 20 cm) of wire with ends stripped
- ✔ switch (as made on pages 10/11)
- ✔ 2 torch bulbs in bulb holders
- ✔ a screwdriver

**1** Make a simple circuit with a switch as on pages 10/11. Close the switch and look closely at what happens.

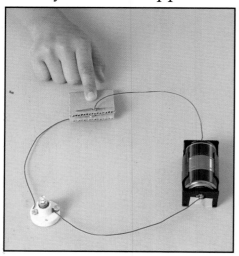

**2** Add a second bulb to the circuit as shown in the picture. Predict what will happen when you close the switch.

**3** Close the switch to see if your prediction was correct. Do both bulbs light up? Do two bulbs light as brightly as one bulb on its own in the circuit?

## In action

Some electrical devices need more batteries to work them than others do. For example, this radio needs four batteries (one is hidden behind the others) but the small torch needs only two.

12

**4** Predict what will happen if you add another battery to the circuit, connected the same way round as the first battery. Test to see if you were right. First try two batteries with one bulb.

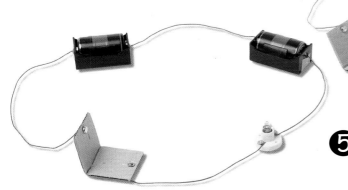

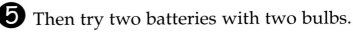

**5** Then try two batteries with two bulbs.

**6** Did the single bulb light more brightly with one battery or two? Did one bulb with one battery light more or less brightly than two bulbs with two batteries?

# Don't stop there

● There are standard symbols for different electrical components which you can use to draw electrical circuits:

| Name of component | Symbol |
|---|---|
| Battery | —\|⊢— |
| Wire | —— |
| Bulb | ⊗ or ⊖ |
| Open switch | —∘⁄ ∘— |
| Closed switch | —∘–∘— |

Draw one of the circuits you made using standard symbols.

● In a circuit of two batteries and one bulb, what happens if you first connect the batteries the same way round, then you turn one round so they are connected in opposite directions? Does the bulb light each time?

# Keep thinking

How many bulbs are there on this circuit drawing? How many batteries? Is the switch open or closed? Will the bulb light?

# In a spin

ELECTRICITY DOESN'T just make light, it can also be used to make things turn round and round. Find out how to set things spinning in this experiment.

## ✓ you will need
- ✓ thick card
- ✓ a small motor
- ✓ paints
- ✓ strong glue
- ✓ tape
- ✓ wooden skewer
- ✓ paper fastener switch
- ✓ 1.5V battery in holder
- ✓ 3 pieces of wire with ends stripped
- ✓ plastic propeller (that fits exactly onto motor shaft)

❶ Make a circuit using the battery in its holder, wires, switch and motor as shown in the picture.

## Keep thinking

Fans and CD players use electric motors. How many other things can you think of that use them as well?

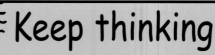

❷ Paint a picture of the front of an aeroplane on the piece of thick card. Make a hole with the skewer where you want the centre of the propeller to be.

**3** Push the motor shaft through this hole and tape the motor to the back of the picture.

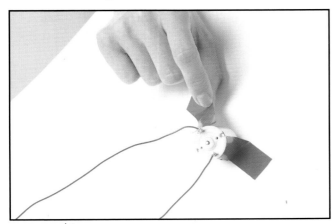

**4** Use strong glue to fix the propeller securely to the motor shaft.

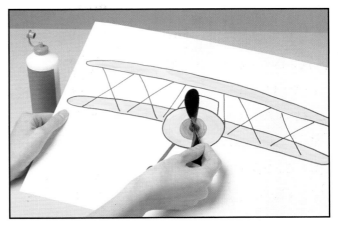

**5** Close the switch. What happens to the propeller? What do you think would happen if you added another battery to the circuit? Test to find out.

# In action

Motors powered by mains electricity are used in large appliances like washing machines and spin driers. This is one of the first spin driers. It was made in Germany in 1929.

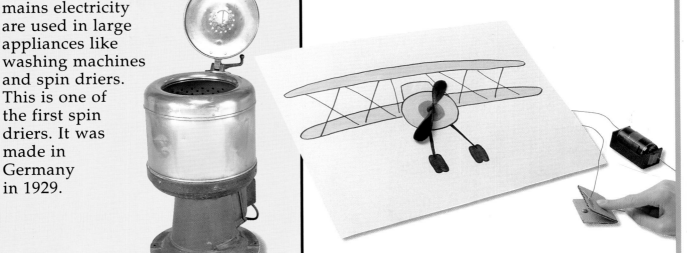

# Don't stop there

● The standard symbol for a motor is (M). Draw the circuit you made using standard symbols.

● Find out if it matters which way round the motor is connected in the circuit by swapping over the wires on its contacts. Does it still work?

# Electric conductors?

**H**AVE YOU NOTICED THAT ALL connection points on a circuit are made of metal? This is because electricity can easily travel through metal. It is called a conductor. A material that electricity cannot travel through is called an insulator. Try this experiment to find out more.

## ✓ you will need
- ✓ 4.5V battery
- ✓ 3.5V bulb in holder
- ✓ 3 pieces of wire with ends stripped
- ✓ various materials to test, e.g. fabrics, paper, card, different types of metal (including iron, nickel and cobalt, if possible), pencil lead (graphite), rubber, plastic, glass, wood, tap water, vinegar

**1** To make your tester, connect the components as shown. The bulb should light up when you hold the two loose ends of wire together.

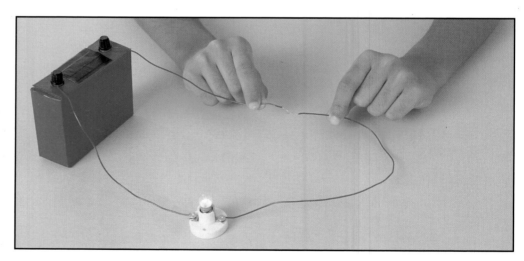

**2** Predict which materials will conduct electricity and which will not. Record your predictions on a table like this one.

| TYPE OF MATERIAL | WILL THE MATERIAL CONDUCT ELECTRICITY? | |
| --- | --- | --- |
| | PREDICTION | RESULT |
| EXAMPLE metal | yes | |
| | | |
| | | |
| | | |
| | | |

**3** Now test each material in turn by using it as the connection between the two loose ends of wire. When you test the water and vinegar, make sure the wire ends do not touch in the liquid as the liquid will no longer be part of the circuit. If the bulb lights up, the material is a conductor.

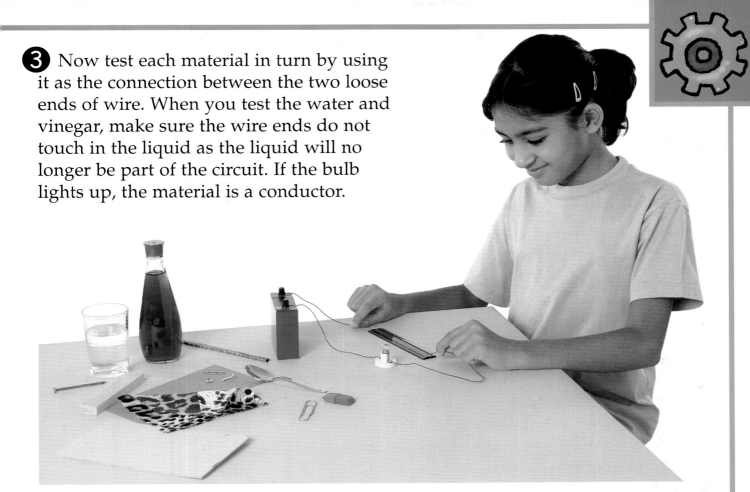

## Keep thinking

Look back at pages 10 and 11 to find out what materials you used to make switches. Which materials are conductors and which are insulators? Why was each type important?

**4** Record your results in the table. Then put all the conductors together and all the insulators together. Are all the metals conductors? Do any other materials conduct electricity? Which material makes a good insulator?

## Don't stop there

● Find out what happens if you dissolve four teaspoons of table salt in warm tap water. Does it conduct electricity?
● Pull the plastic off a small length of insulated wire. Test to find out if the plastic outside or the metal wire inside conducts electricity. What does the wire do? What does the plastic do?

# Resist the flow

Ⓗave you used a dimmer-switch that changes the brightness of a light? Graphite, the material inside pencils, is used in this type of switch. Find out how electricity flows through graphite in this experiment.

**Safety: ask an adult for help with this experiment.**

✅ **you will need**
- ✅ 4.5V battery
- ✅ 3.5V bulb in a holder
- ✅ 3 pieces of wire about 30 cm long with the ends stripped
- ✅ craft knife
- ✅ pencil

❶ Ask an adult to cut the pencil length-wise to show the 'lead' down the middle. This material is really a type of carbon called graphite. It conducts electricity.

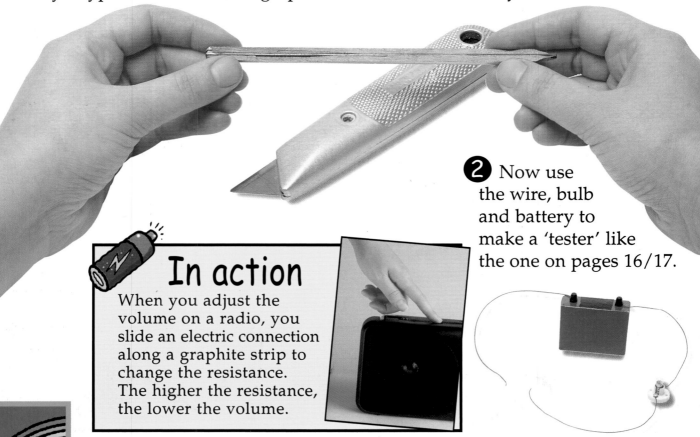

❷ Now use the wire, bulb and battery to make a 'tester' like the one on pages 16/17.

## In action

When you adjust the volume on a radio, you slide an electric connection along a graphite strip to change the resistance. The higher the resistance, the lower the volume.

**3** Hold the ends of the wires on the graphite at either end of the pencil. Gradually slide them closer together along the lead until they are almost touching (but don't let them actually touch). Look closely at the bulb as you do this.

**4** What happens to the bulb as the wires get closer? What is the light like when the wires are far apart? What is it like when they are are almost touching?

**5** Electricity flows through some materials less easily than others. We say they have a higher resistance than those materials that electricity flows through more easily. Resistance increases when electricity has to flow further through a material, too. When you put the wires on the graphite in the pencil when was there the most resistance?

## Don't stop there

Do you think the middle of a pencil crayon will work in the same way? Test to find out.

 **Keep thinking**

Do you think graphite is as good a conductor of electricity as metal wire? Which do you think has more resistance, graphite or wire?

# Connect it up

DO YOUR FRIENDS know the correct symbols for the different electric componetns? Use electric circuits to make a quiz game to test them.

✅ **you will need**
- ✅ piece of thick A4 card
- ✅ wooden skewer
- ✅ 8 paper fasteners
- ✅ 4 self-adhesive stickers
- ✅ marker pen
- ✅ 1.5V battery in a holder
- ✅ thin insulated wire with the ends stripped
- ✅ a friend

- ✅ strong glue
- ✅ 1.5V battery
- ✅ motor
- ✅ 2 torch bulbs
- ✅ bulb holder
- ✅ switch

**1** First make holes for the paper fasteners in the piece of card using the wooden skewer. You need two rows of four holes opposite each other as shown. Attach the fasteners.

**2** Use strong glue to stick the motor, bulb, switch and battery on to the card next to the fasteners on the left as shown in the picture.

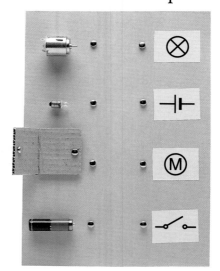

**3** Draw the symbol for a motor, a bulb, a switch and a battery on separate stickers. Stick each one on to the right-hand side of the board – but do NOT put the correct symbol next to the part it represents.

# In action

This game uses a simple electric circuit to test the steadiness of your hand. The aim is to take the wire loop from one end of the wiggly wire to the other without touching it. If the loop touches the wire, it makes a complete circuit, a buzzer sounds and you have to start again.

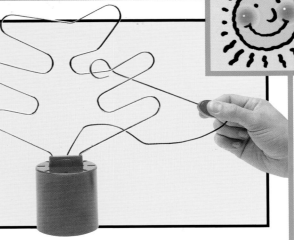

**4** Turn the board over and wind short lengths of wire around the back of the fasteners connecting, each electric part to its correct symbol.

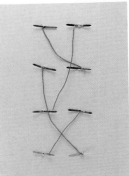

**5** Make a 'tester' using the battery bulb and wire like the one on pages 16/17. Your quiz game is now ready!

**6** Ask a friend to match one of the parts to its symbol by placing one wire from the tester on the paper fastener next to the electric part and the other wire on the fastener next to the symbol he thinks is correct. How will you know if he is right? If he is wrong, he can try again – or let another friend have a go.

# Don't stop there

Design another matching quiz game which uses the same tester as this experiment, for example, match flags to their countries.

# A closer look

HAVE YOU EVER LOOKED really closely at an electric light bulb? How do you think the electricity makes a bulb light up? Take a close look at a bulb and test to find out in this experiment.

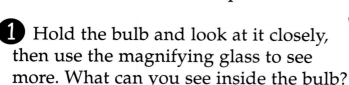
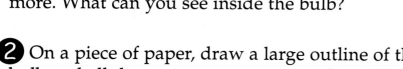
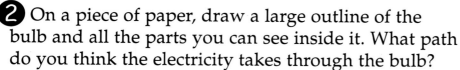

**1** Hold the bulb and look at it closely, then use the magnifying glass to see more. What can you see inside the bulb?

**2** On a piece of paper, draw a large outline of the bulb and all the parts you can see inside it. What path do you think the electricity takes through the bulb?

## Keep thinking

In 1878 Joseph Swan invented the electric light bulb. He took air out of the bulb so the filament did not burn away. Do you think there is air inside the torch bulb you looked at? If not what do you think might be inside it?

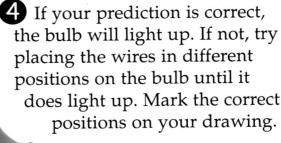

**3** Attach a wire to each end of the battery in the holder. Hold the loose ends of the wires against the bulb where you predict they should go so that the electric current will flow.

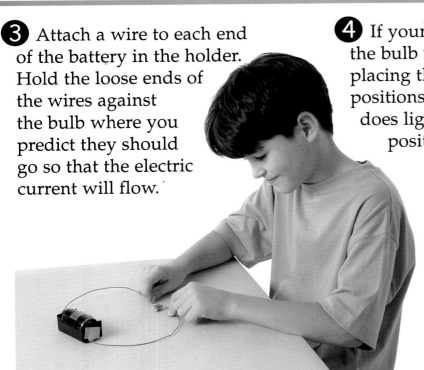

**4** If your prediction is correct, the bulb will light up. If not, try placing the wires in different positions on the bulb until it does light up. Mark the correct positions on your drawing.

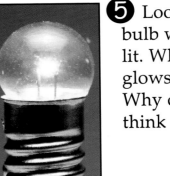

**5** Look at the bulb when it is lit. Which part glows brightly? Why do you think this is?

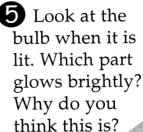

# Don't stop there

The wire that lights up is called the filament. It is very thin so it is difficult for the electric current to flow through it – it has a high resistance. This makes it get white hot and glow. Ask an adult to use tongs to hold some fine wire wool between the two terminals of a 4.5V battery placed in a tray of sand. **DO NOT** try this yourself. What happens? Why?

# In action

In 1879 Thomas Edison designed a light bulb and by 1880 he was manufacturing bulbs like the one on this lamp for people to use in their homes. The filament was made of carbonized cotton. Today filaments are usually made of the metal tungsten which gives a brighter light.

# Alarm bells

ELECTRICITY CAN FLOW EITHER WAY around a circuit, but some electrical machines use components that allow the electric current to flow in only one direction. These are called diodes. Experiment with a diode and make an alarm for a secret treasure box.

**1** First test the buzzer to find out how it works. Hold one wire from the buzzer on each end of the battery. Does the buzzer work? Turn the buzzer round and test it again. Can you hear the buzzer working now? A buzzer is a diode and so it only allows the electricity to flow in one direction.

**2** Now make a security alarm on a secret box. Place the buzzer in the box, make a small hole in the back and push the red wire through. Fold a small piece of foil to the end and tape the wire to the box.

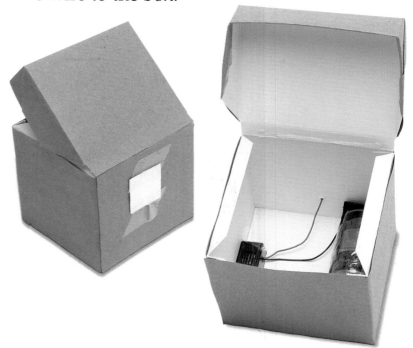

**3** Join the battery to the black wire from the buzzer and tape the holder into the box.

# In action

The lights you see on this music system use Light Emitting Diodes (LEDs). The LEDs flash on and off as the level of the music changes.

**4** Make a small hole above the battery in the lid of the box. Now, with the lid open, cut a piece of wire long enough to reach from the battery through the hole and down to touch the foil end of the red wire. Tape the wire inside the lid.

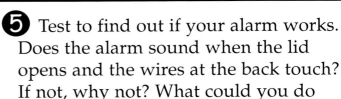

**5** Test to find out if your alarm works. Does the alarm sound when the lid opens and the wires at the back touch? If not, why not? What could you do to make it work? Think about how a diode like your buzzer works.

**6** Put some treasures in your box and close the lid. How will you know if someone tries to look at them?

# Don't stop there

● Draw the circuit for your alarm using standard symbols. The symbol for a buzzer is ⏚.

● Electric current flows from the negative end of a battery round to the positive end. Can you see the – and + on the batteries you have used? Add arrows to your circuit drawing to show the direction the electric current is flowing when the buzzer buzzes!

# Make a magnet

$W$HAT DO A DOORBELL, a loudspeaker and a crane in a scrap-metal yard have in common? They all use a special type of magnet made by electricity. It is called an electromagnet. Make your own magnet in this experiment and use it to see if a material is magnetic.

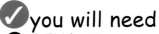 **you will need**
- ✓ 4.5V battery
- ✓ a metal paper clip
- ✓ a stainless steel teaspoon
- ✓ over 1 m of thin insulated wire with the ends stripped
- ✓ small objects for sorting (use the same as on pages 16/17)

## In action

The mouthpiece of a telephone turns the sound of your voice into an electric signal. The electric signal moves a tiny electromagnet in the earpiece of the phone you are speaking to, which turns the electric signal back into sound.

**1** First test your spoon to be sure that it is not a magnet before you start. Do this by touching the paper clip with the spoon. The clip should not be 'attracted' or 'stick' to it.

**2** Make the spoon into a magnet by winding the wire around the spoon at least 40 times, leaving about 30 cm at both ends. Wind each end around a terminal of the battery.

**3** Touch the paper clip again to find out if it is attracted to the spoon now. If it is, you have made an electromagnet.

**4** Use your electromagnet to sort objects into two piles. Label one 'Magnetic' and one 'Not Magnetic'.

Are all the metals magnetic? Are any other materials magnetic?

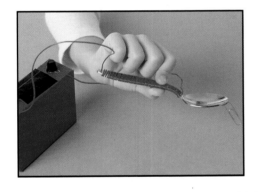

## Don't stop there

- Take one wire off the battery so you break the circuit and the electric current cannot flow. Use the paper clip to test the spoon again. Is it still a magnet? If not, why do you think it has stopped being a magnet?
- Do you think a plastic or wooden spoon will work in the same way? Test to find out.

## Keep thinking

Do all magnetic materials also conduct electricity? Are all the materials that conduct electricity also magnetic? Look back to pages 16/17 to help you decide.

# All together now

OW MANY WAYS DO you use electricity in your bedroom? Use ideas from this book to make a model room with a fan, an alarm and a light in it.

✓ **you will need**
- ✓ cardboard box (e.g. a shoe box)
- ✓ coloured card and scraps of fabric
- ✓ torch bulb in a holder
- ✓ thin insulated wire
- ✓ 3 1.5V batteries
- ✓ marker pens
- ✓ 3 switches
- ✓ propeller
- ✓ sticky tape
- ✓ motor

**1** On a piece of paper design your room and think where you will include a light, a buzzer (as a doorbell or a burglar alarm), and a motor to work a fan.

**2** Make the room out of the box and decorate it with fabric and coloured markers.

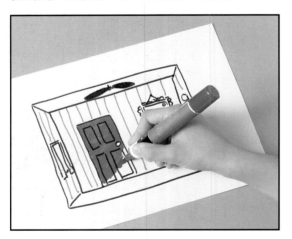

## In action

When the wind blows and turns these windmills around they make machines called turbines spin around and this generates electricity. Turbines can also be powered by water, coal, gas, oil and nuclear reactions.

# Keep thinking

Where does the electricity that flows into your home come from? How can you turn off the electricity in your home?

**3** Draw three separate circuits to show how you will make each component work. Include a switch in each one so you can control the electric current.

**4** Make the circuits and add them to your room.

**5** Does the bulb light up the room? Does the buzzer work? Does the fan go round to cool the room?

# Don't stop there

- Try connecting all electrical components in one circuit. Do they work as well?
- This diagram shows how the mains electricity in a home is placed in 'rings' (shown in blue), with different circuits coming off each ring main, including the ceiling circuits (red). Count all the circuits coming off the ring mains in your living room.

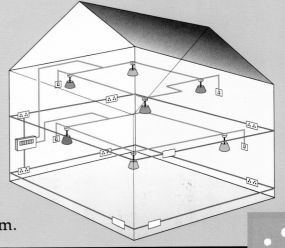

# Glossary

This glossary gives the meaning of each word as it is used in this book.

**Battery** A device used to produce electric current which it pumps around a circuit to make things work.

**Battery operated** A machine that uses electricity provided by batteries to make it work is battery operated.

**Buzzer** An electrical component that makes a buzzing noise when electricity flows through it. A buzzer is a diode so it must be connected in a particular way into a circuit for electricity to flow.

**Circuit** The path of an electric current. For a current to flow, the path must always form a continuous loop or circuit.

**Closed switch** See Switch.

**Conductor** A material that electricity can flow through.

**Copper** A type of metal, red/brown in colour, often used to make the wire for electric circuits.

**Current electricity** Electricity that flows around a circuit.

**Dimmer switch** A type of switch used to control the amount of electricity flowing around a circuit so that, for example, a light bulb can be made to glow brighter or dimmer.

**Diode** An electrical component that allows the current to flow in only one direction.

**Electrical appliances/devices** Machines that use electricity to make them work.

**Electrical components** Small parts, such as bulbs, switches and buzzers, used in electric circuits.

**Electricity** A form of energy when tiny particles, called electrons, flow around a circuit. Electricity is used to heat things, light things and make things work.

**Electromagnet** A type of magnet made when an electric current is flowing in a coil of wire wound around a metal bar.

**Electrons** Very, very tiny particles in all matter.

**Experiment** A fair test done to find out more about something or answer a question. Sometimes called an investigation.

**Filament** The very thin coil inside a light bulb that glows very brightly to give out light when electricity flows through it.

**Generate** To make electricity.

**Graphite** A form of carbon used inside pencils, so it is often called 'pencil lead'. Graphite conducts electricity but not as well as a metal.

**Insulated wire** Electrical wire, which has a material that does not conduct electricity, such as plastic, around it.

**Insulator** A material that electricity cannot flow through.

**Machine** A device or mechanism to make work easier.

**Magnet** A material that attracts certain metals.

**Magnetic** If a magnet attracts a material then the material is magnetic.

**Magnifying glass** A hand-held lens that you look through to make things look bigger and to see details more clearly.

**Materials** Types of matter or 'stuff'. Materials may be solid, liquid or gas.

**Motor** A machine used to turn things, worked by electricity.

**Motor shaft** The spike sticking out from a simple motor that spins around very fast to which other components can be attached to make something move.

**Open switch** See Switch.

**Power station** A place where electricity is made or generated.

**Predict** To guess what will happen in an experiment before doing it.

**Propeller** Two or more specially shaped blades that are attached to a motor shaft. As it spins on the shaft, the propeller moves air or sometimes water.

**Resistance** Resistance is a term used to describe the amount of electricity that flows through a material. A material that allows only small amounts of electricity to flow through it has higher resistance than a material through which electricity flows easily.

**Result(s)** The outcome of an experiment.

**Ring mains** Term used to describe how the sockets on each floor of a building are connected to the mains electricity supply by a circuit in a 'ring'.

**Standard symbols** Simple pictures used when drawing circuits to represent electrical components.

**Static electricity** Electrical energy that cannot flow but stays in one place.

**Switch** An electrical component for controlling the flow of electricity around a circuit. A closed switch completes the circuit and allows an electric current to flow. An open switch breaks the circuit and stops the current flowing.

**Terminals** The places on a battery or electrical device to which wires are connected. Also called 'contacts'.

**Tungsten** A metal that can be heated to a very high temperature before it melts. Thin, coiled pieces of tungsten wire are used to make the filament inside electric light bulbs.

**Turbines** Machines powered by things such as water and wind that produce, or generate, electricity.

**Wire** A thin metal thread, often covered in plastic through which an electric current flows.

**Zinc** A metal used inside some batteries.

# Index